Steam Train Ride

For Christopher, whose passion for steam trains inspired this book.

The author wishes to thank the following people for their help: friends at Strasburg Railroad—Red Shaub, Mel Stimmel, Bill Grager, G. Fred Bartels, and our other friends—librarians of the Yardley-Makefield branch of the Bucks County Free Library; Barbara S. Bates; Michael J. Clarke; Lorraine Durfee; The Reverend N. Dean Evans; Marianne Gilmour; Phelps Johnson; Douglas and Leslie Mott; and employees of Photo-Video of Yardley.

First published in the United States of America in 1991 by Walker Publishing Company, Inc.; first paperback edition published in 1995.

Published simultaneously in Canada by Thomas Allen & Son Canada, Limited, Markham, Ontario

The Library of Congress cataloged the hardcover editions of this book as follows:
Mott, Evelyn Clarke
Steam train ride / Evelyn Clarke Mott.
p.   cm.
Summary: A young boy takes a ride on a steam engine train and learns how it works.
ISBN 0-8027-6995-0 — ISBN 0-8027-6996-9 (reinf.)
1. Railroads—Juvenile literature. [1. Railroads—Trains.]
I. Title.   TF148.M665   1991
625.2′61—dc20   90-49223
CIP
AC
ISBN 0-8027-7452-0 (paper)

design by Georg Brewer

Printed in Hong Kong

2 4 6 8 10 9 7 5 3

Steam Train Ride

Evelyn Clarke Mott

Walker and Company
New York

Christopher loves trains. That is why today is a special day. He is going to see a steam train.

Christopher's eyes widen when he sees the huge railroad yard. The first person he meets is Red, the engineer.

"Will you show me your train?" Christopher asks.

"Of course, young fella," Red says. "Come on up into the cab. I'd like to show you how Engine 89 runs."

"Yes, sir," Christopher says as he steps up into the cab.

"I'm in charge of the engine," Red tells Christopher. "I control the speed of the train and make sure everyone is safe."

Red pulls the brake lever to make the wheels stop. *SHHHHHHHsssss* . . .

"We can't go very far yet." Red says. "Mel and I must get Engine 89 ready before we take it to the station. Come on down, and we'll meet Mel."

"This is the throttle lever. When I pull it back, Engine 89's wheels move."

Christopher feels a bump and hollers with delight when he hears the sound *CHUG-GA, CHUG-GA, CHUGGA, CHUGGA, chugga, chugga.* . . .

"Mel's the fireman. He helps me take care of the train. He oils the engine to keep it running smoothly."

Christopher asks, "Does Mel put out fires on the train?"

"No." Red laughs. "It sounds funny, but Engine 89 needs Mel to make fires, not put them out. Mel shovels coal into the firebox to keep the fire burning."

"The firebox heats the water in the boiler and turns it into steam. Steam makes Engine 89 go."

Red shows Christopher the coaling dock.

"Whew!" Christopher gasps. "Shoveling coal is hard work!"

Red laughs heartily and says, "You would have to shovel a lot more coal to fill Engine 89's tender!"

"What's a tender, Red?"

"The tender is the car that holds coal and water for the engine. Look! Engine 89's tender is stopped at the water tower." Water pours from the spout down into the tender. *Whoosh!*

"I love the signs in the railroad yard," Christopher tells Red. "The railroad crossing sign is my favorite."

"That's a very important sign," Red says, "because it warns people that a train crosses here."

"The *W* on this sign means whistle," Red explains. "When I see this sign, I blow Engine 89's whistle so loud that even the cows know to get off the tracks!"

WOOOOOOOOOO, WOOOOOOOOOO, WOO, WOOOOOOOOO! The train is coming!

"This sign means railroad crossing ahead."

"This funny-looking pole is called a semaphore. Isn't that a mouthful?" Red grins. "Semaphores are like traffic lights. They tell me whether Engine 89 should stop or go."

"It's time to bring Engine 89 to the railroad station," Red says. "See you soon!"

Christopher hurries to the ticket office. "One ticket, please."

He waits inside the station for Engine 89.

WOOOOOOOOO, WOOOOOOOOO, WOO, WOOOOOOOOO! Here comes the train!

*S*HHHHHHHsssss . . . The wheels stop. Black
smoke and clouds of steam hide the cab. When the
steam clears, Christopher sees the number 89 and
leaps off the bench. *"Hooray!"*

Bill is the conductor. He is in charge of the train ride. Bill helps Red back up the engine to couple on the passenger cars. When the cars are safely hooked up to the engine, Bill shouts, *"All aboard!"*

It's time to get on the train!

"Ticket, please." Bill looks to see where Christopher is going and punches his ticket.

CHUG-GA, CHUG-GA, CHUGGA,
CHUGGA, chugga, chugga . . .

The train starts slowly . . .

. . . and then goes faster.

It's fun to look out of the window as the train rumbles on.

Christopher sees sheep,

horses and cows,

mules,

people,

and farms.

Red blows the whistle and then a bell rings,
DING, DING, DING, DING, DING, DING. The lights on
the railroad crossing sign flash. The gate drops
across the road. After the train passes, the gate goes
up and the lights shut off.

Engine 89 stops at other railroad stations to let people on and off. This is Cherry Hill Station.

The train gently rocks as it winds its way along the tracks. Christopher sways as he listens to the *clickety-clack* of the wheels.

Red pulls the brake lever. *SHHHHHHHsssss* . . . Engine 89 is back at the station.

"Good-bye, Red. Good-bye, Mel. Good-bye, Bill," Christopher says. "So long, Engine 89. What a great day!"

As Christopher leaves, Engine 89 whistles a long, wonderful WOOOOOOO-OOOOO. . . .